BASEBALL SMARTS

100 Questions to Measure Your Baseball IQ

When Watching a Baseball Game, How Much Are You Missing?

Darren Gurney

COACHES CHOICE™

ISBN: 978-1-60679-437-1
Library of Congress Control Number: 2018947988
Cover design: Cheery Sugabo
Book layout: Cheery Sugabo
Front cover photos: W. Scott McGill/Shutterstock.com and Eugene Onischenko/
          Shutterstock.com
Back cover photo: 3Dalia/Shutterstock.com

Coaches Choice
P.O. Box 1828
Monterey, CA 93942
www.coacheschoice.com

Other Books by Darren Gurney

Covering All the Bases: The Ultimate Baseball Handbook

101 Defensive Baseball Drills

"Baseball is like church.
Many attend,
but few understand."

—Wes Westrum, San Francisco Giants

Dedication

To the Japanese people who have changed my life forever

Acknowledgments

I would like to acknowledge Dr. James Peterson and his team at Coaches Choice. Their generosity, commitment to excellence, and professionalism have made for a special relationship that I greatly cherish. I look forward to working on more projects with Coaches Choice in the coming years.

Contents

Introduction

A fellow coach recently asked me during a baseball trip to Japan, what percentage of baseball do you think you know? Before answering, I thought to myself, I have been playing baseball since I was six years old, attended numerous baseball camps as a teen, played on countless summer baseball teams, watched thousands of MLB games, played high school baseball and subsequently four years of NCAA baseball, and then played baseball for 11 years after my college years.

I also considered my experience coaching high school and college baseball for the past 26 years. During these years, I have attended numerous coaches clinics and conventions and have had dozens of in-depth baseball discussions with coaches at all competitive levels. In addition, I reflected on reading hundreds of baseball books and having two books of my own published. Furthermore, I was involved in filming four instructional DVDs, as well as 30 other Internet-based baseball videos, which required considerable research and planning within baseball fundamentals. I have also been running camps and clinics throughout the year for the past 20 years that require much baseball study and reflection.

My initial impulse was to provide an answer, reflecting that I know a large percentage of baseball, having spent almost my whole life in and around baseball. But, then I realized that his question asked: *what percentage of baseball do I know?* (Not what percentage do I know compared to other people.) So, I began to think—do I know 70 percent, 50 percent, 30 percent, or some other percentage of the vast breadth of baseball's millions of intricacies? And then I remembered something that humbled me...*The Baseball Case Book*.

Every year, new situations occur in baseball that require umpires and rules committees to discuss and decide on hundreds of random, bizarre cases. National and state federations publish these new cases annually in a book. Not to be confused with the mammoth baseball rules book, the case book can bring any baseball aficionado to his knees.

Ultimately, I never answered the question. Still now, I am not sure what my answer is. How many team sports are played without a clock and, in turn, do not restrict the length and number of varied situations that can happen in a given game? In what other sports are the playing areas and contours of every field different, which creates more possible scenarios? How many other sports have to publish a case book every year to address these hypothetical situations? In no other sport or field of industry are there so many twists, turns, and depth of knowledge/information. Perhaps this is a self-realization you have come to and reason why you are reading this book.

Please keep in mind that this book only contains 100 elements of baseball that I deem worth knowing as a fan, player, or coach. The beauty of baseball (and life) is that if we pay attention, we get to learn new things with every game and day. As with any endeavor, the optimal way to learn is by doing. So, read this book, watch baseball games, pick up a copy of a case book, and learn. Most of all, make sure you have fun watching games and discussing them with other people.

And when you think you are ready, you can *Catch a Game With Coach Gurney* for a small fee. To book viewing a game with me or to ask a random, baseball-related question, please send an email to: CoachGurney@gmail.com.

PART 1:
QUESTIONS

Q: 1. What are eight different ways a batter can advance to first base (in the scorebook)?

Q: 2. What is a "dropped third strike"? [When can a batter advance to first base after striking out?]

Q: 3. Why do they water the infield dirt before the game?

Q: 4. What is "catcher's interference"? [What is the penalty? How does it affect a hitter's batting average?]

Q: 5. What is a "pitch-up" (not a "pitch-out")? [When is it used?]

Q: 6. What is a catcher's balk? [What is the penalty?]

Q: 7. What is the lane on the first baseline used for? [What rule does it deal with?]

Q: 8. What is a "delayed steal"? [How does a runner execute it?]

9. When taking a (primary) lead off first base, where might you see a base runner's eyes looking besides the pitcher or third base coach? Why?

 10. Why does the shortstop sometimes signal to the second baseman with an open or closed mouth (a hidden signal with his lips open/together behind his glove)?

 11. How does the catcher signal that he is throwing down to second base on the last warm-up pitch in between innings? [At the youth level, catchers typically yell "coming down."]

 12. What is the "daylight play"? [You may see the shortstop quickly flash his glove to the pitcher.]

 13. Why does the pitcher sometimes point at the shortstop, when a new batter stands in to hit (or wiggle his hand with the pinkie finger and thumb extended)?

14. Why does the catcher, coach, and/or pitcher cover his mouth with his glove, when he speaks at the mound?

15. Why and when does the catcher sometimes run down the first baseline behind the batter?

 16. Why do catchers sometimes have tape or nail polish on the fingers of their right hand?

 17. Why do catchers sometimes flash only one signal for the pitcher to see and other times flash a series of signals?

 18. Why will a coach in the bullpen sometimes take his hat off and wave it so that the manager in the dugout can see it from hundreds of feet away?

 19. What is the difference between a "safety squeeze" and a "suicide squeeze" bunt?

 20. How far is the catcher's throw from home plate to second base? [Hint: If you are a good math student and know that there is a 90-degree right angle involved, you may be able to figure it out.]

21. What is a "balk-move" (not what is a "balk")?

22. What is the call/ruling when a batter hits a line drive off the pitcher's rubber/plate that flies into the third base dugout? What if a batter hits a line drive off second base, and the ball flies directly into the third base dugout?

 23. Why do batters sometimes remove the lines (back line) in the batter's box?

 24. What is the "infield fly rule"? [When is it called (which specific situations) and why does the rule exist?]

 25. Why do players avoid stepping on chalk foul lines?

 26. When a catcher gets hit with a foul tip, why will you see the umpire clean off home plate and/or walk a new ball out to the pitcher?

 27. Why will the pitcher sometimes keep looking in at the catcher after a pitch signal has already been given?

Q: 28. What signals will a pitcher show to his catcher in between innings to alert him as to which type of warm-up pitch is coming?

Q: 29. Why will a base runner on first base sometimes look in toward home plate as he dashes to second base and other times not look in on his dash to second base?

Q: 30. If a switch-hitter gets into the batter's box versus a switch-handed (ambidextrous) pitcher, who has to declare first which side they are pitching or hitting from?

Q: 31. Why will a hitter sometimes smell his bat in the batter's box?

Q: 32. What is an "inside move" or "step over"?

Q: 33. What is and provide an example of verbal obstruction?

Q: 34. What is the proper umpire call when the infield is playing in on the grass and the batter hits a ground ball that hits a base runner leading off first base?

Q: 35. In the USA, how many warm-up pitches is a pitcher allowed to throw before an inning begins? Is it the same number throughout the game?

Q: 36. If a player misses a coach's signals, how can he signal to show that he wants them repeated?

Q: 37. What is the purpose of the little white pouch on the dirt part of the back of the pitcher's mound?

Q: 38. How do defensive teams defend or guard against a bunt?

Q: 39. Why are there so many left-handed first basemen?

Q: 40. Why do pitchers wear a jacket when running the bases?

Q: 41. Aside from defending against a possible bunt, why does the third baseman sometimes jog in and out a few steps in the middle of an inning?

Q: 42. Why can a manager call "time-out" and argue for a longer, more arbitrary amount of time than a coach in any other sport?

Q: 43. What should the on-deck batter be doing, while waiting for his turn at bat?

Q: 44. What is the difference between a drag bunt and a push bunt?

Q: 45. Why would a fielder purposely drop a pop-up or fly ball?

Q: 46. When or why would a runner tag up at first base?

Q: 47. How should a fielder grip a ball before throwing it?

Q: 48. Why might an infielder or outfielder play a ground ball differently, if it is hit by the lead-off hitter, as opposed to the fifth batter in the lineup?

Q: 49. Why does the catcher only sometimes stand in the on-deck circle, waiting his turn to hit wearing shin guards on his legs?

Q: 50. Why do middle-infielders (shortstops and second basemen) wear the smallest gloves/mitts on the field?

Q: 51. What is the *backdoor play*?

Q: 52. What is a *Baltimore chop*?

Q: 53. What is a *Texas Leaguer*?

Q: 54. What is *the neighborhood play* and will instant replay make it obsolete?

Q: 55. What is a *double-switch*?

Q: 56. What is the rag or giant ChapStick-looking tube that hitters often rub on their bats before hitting?

Q: 57. Why do so many pitchers get hurt and require arm surgery?

58. How can a manager protest a game (file a protest)?

 59. What is a first-and-third defense?

 60. Why would a MLB manager expect a base runner to sprint from second base to home plate on a base hit, especially with two outs?

 61. Why might a MLB manager not expect a hitter to sprint to first base after hitting a routine ground ball on the infield, no matter how many outs there are?

 62. Can a pitcher spit on his hand and then "rub up" the baseball? Can he rub the ball in the dirt? Can he blow on his hand?

 63. Why will a hitter sometimes tap the top of his helmet in the middle or beginning of an at bat?

 64. Why might a batter be hit by a pitch and not be awarded first base on a "hit by pitch"?

Q: 65. What is *defensive indifference*?

Q: 66. What is a *slide-step*?

Q: 67. What does it mean to *step in the bucket*?

Q: 68. Name four types of fastballs.

Q: 69. What is a *hanger*?

Q: 70. Why do catchers often look up at the hitter's face and eyeballs while giving the pitch signals?

Q: 71. Why are there so many players with arm and leg guards?

Q: 72. How come pitchers rarely throw complete games?

Q: 73. Why are there so many strikeouts in the modern MLB?

Q: 74. Is it wrong for a team to keep scoring and stealing bases, when they have a large lead?

Q: 75. What/where is the strike zone?

Q: 76. Why do players slide headfirst into first base?

Q: 77. Why do players slide headfirst into home plate?

Q: 78. Why do players leave their fielding gloves in a specific location in the dugout?

Q: 79. What is a "small ball" game strategy?

Q: 80. Why would a catcher purposely not catch a pitch?

Q: 81. What is a *check-swing*?

Q: 82. What is the hidden ball trick?

Q: 83. What is *double-play depth*?

Q: 84. What is an *unassisted double play*?

Q: 85. Who decides which pitch to throw: the catcher, pitcher, or coach?

Q: 86. What is a *double-cut*?

Q: 87. Why do infielders sometimes play on or move closer to the foul lines?

Q: 88. What is the *five-man infield*?

89. What is an *over-shift* or *shift*?

 90. What is an *unintentional intentional walk*?

 91. Why would a pitcher want to vary his timing and not deliver pitches with the same pace every time?

 92. Why might hitters (or their coaches) decide that they should "take a strike" before swinging?

 93. Why are coaches often seen looking at binders in the dugout?

 94. Why do infield cutoff men sometimes catch throws from the outfielders and other times purposely let them go by?

 95. What is a *walking lead*?

 96. What does it mean to *go up the ladder*?

97. How does a pitcher earn a *save*?

 98. Why are the players always chewing?

 99. What is a *12-6 curveball*?

 100. What is *pepper*?

PART 2:
ANSWERS

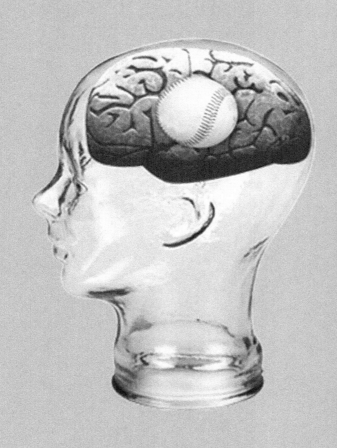

1. What are eight different ways a batter can advance to first base (in the scorebook)?

- Single (1B)
- Base on balls (BB/walk)
- Dropped third strike (K/E-2)
- Catcher's interference (C-Int.)
- Error (E)
- Fielder's choice (FC)
- Hit by pitch (HBP)
- Intentional walk (IBB)

2. What is a "dropped third strike"? [When can a batter advance to first base after striking out?]

Daniel Moxey

A dropped third strike occurs when there is a wild pitch or passed ball by the catcher on a strikeout. The batter who has struck out can run and advance to first base, if it is unoccupied, or if there are two outs. Quite often at youth levels, the batter runs to first base not knowing the rules and/or the catcher throws to first base, because he does not know the rules. Because this is a live ball situation, an errant throw by the catcher can enable other base runners to advance.

At the major-league level, many batters are too lazy or unwilling to sprint down to first base when it is unoccupied in this situation. However, on strikeouts, when the pitch rolls to the backstop or scoots away from the catcher, batters will often successfully advance to first base.

Q: 3. Why do they water the infield dirt before the game?

stephenkirsh/Shutterstock.com

A: Field maintenance is an area that has greatly improved and has taken on a tremendous amount of focus in the modern era of baseball. With grounds crews, newer stadiums, and research concerning optimum field-playing conditions, baseball fields have never been so impeccably cared for as they are today.

After batting practice, the infield dirt is dragged with mats and later sprayed with water. Water is used so that the field is not too dusty and is the proper consistency. Historically, teams watered the infield more than usual to slow down the base paths so that speedy base runners could be kept at bay. In addition, the height of grass would also be strategically designed to either enhance or inhibit the bunting of opponents/ home team. In fact, on occasion, some players during pregame warm-ups can be seen rolling balls from home plate down the third-base line to gauge how the contours and slope of the field may affect a bunted ball.

Modern fields are built with underground drainage systems, and moisture levels are checked regularly. With large tarps and many hands to pull them on and off the field, a relatively large percentage of games are played with intermittent rainy conditions. Teams use various breaks in the game, mostly in between innings, to smooth the dirt on the infield, and replace bases with freshly painted/new ones. This practice has often been integrated into in-game entertainment with the playing of (loud) music and other activities designed to be enjoyable for spectators.

Q: 4. What is "catcher's interference"? [What is the penalty? How does it affect a hitter's batting average?]

A: Catcher's interference occurs when the catcher interferes with the batter's swing. He may be set up too close in his stance to the batter, or the batter may have a longer than typical swing and make contact with the catcher's glove, shin guard, or other body part, which negatively impacts affects his attempt to hit the baseball.

At the youth and high school levels, coaches will often prompt their catcher to move up or back in the catcher's box to prevent this situation from happening. On rare occasions, however, hitters have non-conventional swings that cause their bats to swing back further than typical. Coaches and catchers should be cognizant of this possible scenario.

By rule, catcher's interference is ruled an error on the catcher; no plate appearance for the batter; the runners advance only if forced. It is interesting to note that Jacoby Ellsbury, currently a center fielder for the New York Yankees, has reached base an MLB career record 31 times due to catcher's interference [Tim Kurtzian, ESPN broadcast: September 2017].

5. What is a "pitch-up" (not a "pitch-out")? [When is it used?]

thomas m spindle/Shutterstock.com

Not to be confused with a pitch-out, a pitch-up is used when the defensive team suspects, on a specific pitch, that there may be a suicide squeeze bunt or straight steal of home plate. A pitch-out will take the catcher out of the home plate area, which will make him late to apply the tag to an incoming base runner. In contrast, a pitch-up is utilized where the pitch is thrown at the strike zone, but two to three feet above the batter's waist. It should be thrown high enough so that the batter cannot make contact with the pitch, yet not so high that the catcher cannot successfully glove the baseball.

Q: 6. What is a catcher's balk? [What is the penalty?]

Aspen Photo/Shutterstock.com

 Technically, a "catcher's balk" is catcher's obstruction, which is deemed an illegal pitch. As a result, it is treated like a pitcher's balk. When it occurs, the umpire calls time-out and has the base runners advance one base each.

By rule, the catcher may not leave the catcher's box, or catching assigned area, at the time of the pitch. In the case of a steal situation, the catcher may be inclined to come out of the box to receive a pitch-out. In addition, if the catcher senses that a bunt or steal of home is happening, he may try to get an early jump on the play and vacate his area too soon. If he does this before the pitch is delivered, a dead ball is ruled, and each of the runners advances one base.

7. What is the lane on the first baseline used for? [What rule does it deal with?]

Toronto-Images.Com/Shutterstock.com

 On an MLB diamond, NCAA field, and a properly prepared high school field, there is a lane drawn for the last 45 feet of the first baseline. This running lane provides a clear path for the runner to approach first base. It should be noted that the lane does not allow him to run intentionally in the vision-line of the first baseman, who is receiving a possible throw from the catcher or pitcher. This lane becomes a factor on several plays within the context of a baseball game, including fielded bunts and dropped third strikes, in which the catcher must field and quickly throw to the first baseman. If the runner veers out of this lane, he is called out. This can be a difficult call for the home plate umpire, given that he is almost 90 feet away and is watching the timing of the throw and whether the runner's foot touches first base before the ball arrives. At the MLB level, a four-umpire system is used, which enables the first base umpire to handle the safe/out call at first base.

Q: 8. What is a "delayed steal"? [How does a runner execute it?]

Eric Broder Van Dyke/Shutterstock.com

A: The delayed steal play is one in which the base runner takes off to steal later than normal, a tactic that is designed to surprise the defense. In this situation, he takes a secondary lead, which attempts to fool the defense into thinking no steal play is occurring. After taking his second or third shuffle step of the secondary lead, he sprints for the next base. This play is especially effective, if either the catcher is falling to his knees after receiving each pitch or the middle infielders are not hustling toward second base after every pitch.

Another type of delayed steal involves the base runner sprinting to the next base just as the catcher is throwing the ball back to the pitcher after a given pitch. While this strategy is more difficult to execute, it can be used by base runners with tremendous running speed or if the defensive team gets lackadaisical.

9. When taking a (primary) lead off first base, where might you see a base runner's eyes looking besides the pitcher or third base coach? Why?

Dennis Ku/Shutterstock.com

[Note: Players are taught to stay on the base or keep a foot on the base while looking at the third base coach's signals, finding where the ball is, or looking at/ speaking with the first base coach.]

At the major-league level, talented base stealers will quickly peek at the catcher's signals, while taking their primary lead. This is not an easy task as they must make sure not to get picked off, as they briefly take their eyes off the pitcher. In addition, they must time their quick glare at the catcher properly, as he flashes signals to the pitcher only for a second or two. The purpose of this peek is to see if an off-speed pitch is coming, which will result in the pitcher's delivery to home plate to be slower. If such a scenario unfolds, his ability to steal second base successfully will be enhanced. It should be emphasized that only highly skilled, aggressive base stealers will look in for catcher signals, while leading at first base.

10. Why does the shortstop sometimes signal to the second baseman with an open or closed mouth (a hidden signal with his lips open/together behind his glove)?

Lizzie Short

With a runner on first base and a possible threat of an attempted stolen base, the middle infielders must communicate with each other concerning who will be covering second base. On a stolen-base attempt, one fielder will hold his position, while the other will sprint over to second base to receive the throw from the catcher.

Prior to the pitch, the second baseman or shortstop will cover his lips with his fielding glove and turn to his middle infielder-partner and either open or close his mouth. With his mouth and lips closed, he is signaling that he is going to cover the base. Closed lips means "mine." When the signal is an open-mouth, it means that his partner will cover the base.

Typically, the decision as to who covers the base is determined by which field location the fielders or coach anticipate where the batter is likely to hit the baseball. For example, a right-handed batter will more commonly hit to the shortstop area. Therefore, the shortstop should cover his position and let the second baseman race over to the base. There are exceptions to this rule, such as the offense putting a hit-and-run on or a hard throwing pitcher. In both of these cases, a right-handed batter is more likely to hit the ball toward the second base area or the "4-hole." For this reason, it is important that the middle infielders communicate on every pitch during an at-bat with a runner on first base.

11. How does the catcher signal that he is throwing down to second base on the last warm-up pitch in between innings? [At the youth level, catchers typically yell "coming down."]

Lizzie Short

At the NCAA and professional levels of play, catchers do not yell "coming down" before throwing to second base in between innings. Instead, from a squatted position, they extend both arms horizontally outward. The middle infielders know at this point that they should cover second base. In large, noisy stadiums screaming "coming down" or using verbal communications is ineffective.

Q: 12. What is the "daylight play"? [You may see the shortstop quickly flash his glove to the pitcher.]

Daniel Moxey

A: The daylight play is a synchronized pickoff throw to second base that attempts to nab a base runner with an aggressive lead. The name derives from the notion that if the pitcher can see daylight in between the base runner and the shortstop, who is moving toward covering the base, then he should make a pickoff throw to second base. The shortstop will "flash leather" (his glove) to signal to the pitcher that he is ready for a pickoff throw.

13. Why does the pitcher sometimes point at the shortstop, when a new batter stands in to hit (or wiggle his hand with the pinkie finger and thumb extended)?

Lizzie Short

 When a runner gets to first base with less than two outs, it is customary for the pitcher to signal to one of his middle infielders that he will be throwing the ball to him on a pitch hit right back to the pitcher, a batted ball known as a "comebacker." If the shortstop is playing deep in the hole closer to third base, the pitcher will signal to the second baseman that he will throw to him to turn a possible double play. More commonly, the pitcher will signal to and throw to the shortstop to turn the double play. With the tendency of many hitters to pull the ball, resulting in teams shifting the positions of their infielders, this change in defensive alignments may alter to whom the pitcher throws the ball on a potential double play, comebacker.

Q: 14. Why does the catcher, coach, and/or pitcher cover his mouth with his glove, when he speaks at the mound?

Aspen Photo/Shutterstock.com

A: During televised games, players often cover their mouths with their gloves or hands when communicating during conferences at the pitcher's mound. Discussions centering upon how to pitch a particular batter or the game plan for the infield can be revealed to the offensive team, if their lips are somehow read, e.g., via a television monitor. In many cases, especially at the lower competitive levels of play, players and coaches are often overly paranoid and unnecessarily cover their mouths.

15. Why and when does the catcher sometimes run down the first baseline behind the batter?

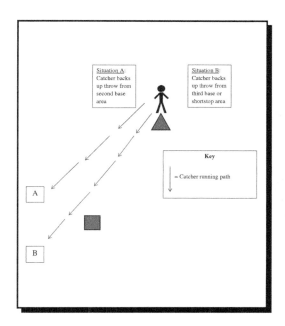

Situation A:
Catcher backs up throw from second base area

Situation B:
Catcher backs up throw from third base or shortstop area

Key

= Catcher running path

A

B

Keeton Gale/Shutterstock.com

The catcher runs down the first baseline to back up infielder throws to first base on routine ground balls hit on the infield. When done properly, the catcher takes an angle that would realistically be on the same line as the throw. A throw from third base requires that the catcher run toward the right-field line, whereas the angle of a throw from the second baseman's area does not require the catcher to run a full 90 feet to first base. The catcher should also back up first base on potential throws from the outfield to first base in case an outfielder throws behind a runner to first base. Catchers will not back up first base, if there is a man on second base or third base, since they must be in position to cover the home plate area in the case of a play at home. Given the fact that catchers wear heavy equipment and cumbersome shin guards, running 70 to 120 feet to back up first base throughout the game is not an easy task.

Q: 16. Why do catchers sometimes have tape or nail polish on the fingers of their right hand?

Gurganusimages/Shutterstock.com

A: During night games, pitchers often struggle to see and read the signals of catchers. Some pitchers have poor eyesight, while others simply struggle to see the catcher's fingers at nighttime from 60 feet away. As a result, many catchers will use white nail polish or tape around their fingers, so that pitchers have a better chance to see their signals. Otherwise, the pitcher may throw the wrong pitch and "cross up" the catcher. When this situation happens, the catcher will struggle to catch the pitch, since he will not be expecting the ball to break or run a certain way.

17. Why do catchers sometimes flash only one signal for the pitcher to see and other times flash a series of signals?

Tom Wang/Shutterstock.com

When giving signals to the pitcher, the catcher is always concerned about the opponent stealing signs. Sometimes, as the catcher puts his signals down between his legs, he will look up at the batter to make sure that he is not peeking down to take a look to see what pitch is coming. With a runner on second base, the catcher will flash multiple signals, so that the runner cannot figure out which pitch is coming and either relay the pitch to the hitter or steal a base on an off-speed pitch. In some cases, the catcher will flash four to six signals, but only one particular signal (e.g., the second one) will be live. The urge to steal a catcher's signals can be pervasive. For example, during the 2017 season, the New York Yankees and Boston Red Sox played games in which the Red Sox were accused of using an Apple watch or cell phone to steal and relay signals into the dugout and then on to the batter.

18. Why will a coach in the bullpen sometimes take his hat off and wave it so that the manager in the dugout can see it from hundreds of feet away?

Lizzie Short

When the bullpen coach takes his hat off his head, he is signaling to the manager and pitching coach that the pitcher warming up in the bullpen is ready to enter the game. As an alternative, major league managers use a telephone to communicate with the bullpen coach to make sure that a pitcher is warm and throwing effectively. This phone call is quite often handled by the pitching coach in the dugout.

Q: 19. What is the difference between a "safety squeeze" and a "suicide squeeze" bunt?

Daniel M. Silva/Shutterstock.com

A: A safety squeeze bunt is simply a sacrifice bunt in which the batter is trying to move the runner over. In this instance, the runner on third base must get a good "read " on whether he will be able to score, based on the effectiveness of the bunt and the defensive positioning of the infielders.

In contrast, a suicide squeeze bunt is a more aggressive strategy to score a runner from third base with a bunt. During a suicide squeeze bunt, the runner on third base breaks for home, before the pitcher releases the ball to home plate. In this scenario, it is imperative that the batter make contact with the ball during the bunt play. Otherwise, the runner will be out at home plate. Defenses may be on guard for a suicide squeeze bunt, depending on the score of the game, the batter at the plate, and the philosophy of the offensive team. The suicide squeeze bunt, along with the straight steal of home, is among the most exciting plays in all of baseball.

20. How far is the catcher's throw from home plate to second base? [Hint: If you are a good math student and know that there is a 90-degree right angle involved, you may be able to figure it out.]

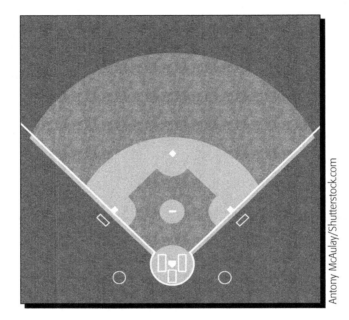

Antony McAulay/Shutterstock.com

 Home plate to second base measures 127 feet 3 3/8 inches. This distance can be calculated by using the Pythagorean theorem in which two right angles of a triangle can be squared and added together to figure out the length of the third angle.

In terms of training catchers to throw effectively, it is important that coaches have this distance properly measured on practice fields. The measurement of bases, pitching rubbers, and bullpen mounds has been manipulated over the years to give home teams an advantage. For example, over the years, several home teams have been accused of changing the distance of their bullpen mounds to throw off opposing pitchers before they enter a game. More often than not, having those pitchers warm up in a bullpen that is 59 or 61 feet from home plate can be just enough to throw them off when they throw on the game mound from 60'6". This maneuver by home teams has been viewed as gamesmanship by some and "bush league" by others. It is very hard for the visiting team to recognize and identify these acts of trickery. As a result, some coaches carry a tape measure with them to all road games.

21. What is a "balk-move" (not what is a "balk")?

Bill Florence/Shutterstock.com

A balk occurs when the pitcher deceives the base runner. A balk move is when a pitcher uses subtle movements that an umpire cannot detect, which deceives the base runner. The pitcher may slightly flinch or quickly move his knees, ankles, or feet in such a manner that confuses the base runner. This confusion is aimed at picking off the base runner or holding him close to the base, so he cannot steal and advance to the next base. Given that umpires have to watch so many different actions on the field, a slight lift of the heel by the pitcher can often go undetected by umpires. For example, with a runner on first base, a right-handed pitcher may slightly lift his left heel before making a pick-off attempt to first base. This lifting of the left heel will convince the base runner that the pitcher is delivering a pitch to home plate. However, he may then deceive the runner by picking off to first base. Technically, a pitcher lifting the left heel is a balk, and the runner should be awarded second base. On the other hand, the umpire may not catch such a "balk move."

Q: 22. What is the call/ruling when a batter hits a line drive off the pitcher's rubber/plate that flies into the third base dugout? What if a batter hits a line drive off second base, and the ball flies directly into the third base dugout?

Brian Eichhorn/Shutterstock.com

A: As noted in the introduction, the case book outlines and addresses the dozens of new, bizarre scenarios that occur annually in baseball games. While the cases may seem trivial or unlikely to ever occur, they are real and do actually occur in future games. A line drive that hits off the pitcher's plate or rubber and lands in foul territory is a foul ball by ruling. A line drive that hits off second base that ricochets into the stands is ruled a double. These examples demonstrate the enormity of different cases that can occur on baseball fields of which umpires, coaches, and players must be aware.

Q: 23. Why do batters sometimes remove the lines (back line) in the batter's box?

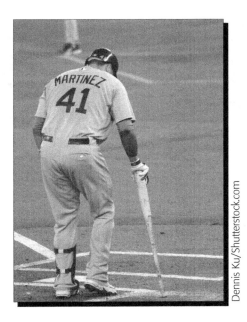

Dennis Ku/Shutterstock.com

A: Hitters sometimes enter the batter's box and remove the rear white lines with their feet. The purpose of this is so they can stand further back and not be illegally out of the batter's box. This tactic gives them the maximum distance and time to see the ball from the pitcher. In particular, since a hard-throwing pitcher can make it challenging for a hitter to have time to hit the ball, this strategy maximizes a hitter's chance to succeed.

By rule, a hitter should be called out if he makes contact with the baseball with either foot out of the batter's box. Umpires, however, rarely make this call. Conversely, with an off-speed pitcher throwing, it may be advantageous for the batter to move up to the front of the batter's box. This movement is commonly seen at the youth level, when pitchers start throwing curve balls. Unless a coach points it out, however, umpires will rarely enforce this rule.

During a major league game, you may notice some players standing inside toward the plate, while others stand away from the plate. These decisions are often based on whether a hitter feels that he has strong or weak plate coverage, based on the nature of his swing. Because some hitters like the ball inside, they will therefore crowd or move in on the plate. In contrast, other batters like the ball a bit away from them. As a result, they will stand off the plate a significant amount.

24. What is the "infield fly rule"? [When is it called (which specific situations) and why does the rule exist?]

Bill Florence/Shutterstock.com

The infield fly is called with runners on first and second base or with the bases loaded, with less than two outs on a pop-up on the infield/shallow outfield area. The rule does not apply on foul balls or bunted balls, on which runners may advance at their own risk. The rule exists to prevent the defense from intentionally dropping a pop-up to turn a double or triple play. An umpire should point skyward when the ball is at its apex and call "infield fly, the batter is out if fair." This rule went into effect in 1895.

25. Why do players avoid stepping on chalk foul lines?

Lizzie Short

Eric Broder Van Dyke/Shutterstock.com

All-in-all, baseball players have a reputation for being superstitious. Perhaps the most widely followed superstition is not stepping on the chalk, the white lines on the first and third base lines. Some players go as far as to jump over the foul lines, while others have alternative superstitions that govern their behavior. These irrational behaviors include eating certain foods, stepping on the field at a certain minute, and wearing specific undergarments, as well as various other peculiarities.

26. When a catcher gets hit with a foul tip, why will you see the umpire clean off home plate and/or walk a new ball out to the pitcher?

DarioZg/Shutterstock.com

Catchers and umpires have a working relationship behind home plate. There is etiquette and chemistry that they aspire to attain. When either gets hit by a foul ball or wild pitch, the other will walk toward the pitcher to give him time to shake off getting hit by the ball. Quite often, catchers are hit by foul tips and umpires will get a new baseball and walk it out to the pitcher. In addition, he may take out his brush and clean off home to buy some time. Similarly, when the umpire gets hit, it is common for the catcher to ask if he is okay and walk out toward the pitcher. This catcher/umpire relationship is important, given that they will spend two or more hours on the field together. Likewise, if a catcher wants to question a strike call, he should do so in a polite manner, without turning around and showing up the umpire.

27. Why will the pitcher sometimes keep looking in at the catcher after a pitch signal has already been given?

Keeton Gale/Shutterstock.com

Pitchers and catchers have to be mindful of offensive teams stealing their pitch signals. Even after a pitcher receives the signal, he may continue staring at the catcher and use a strategy of false shake-offs. These are movements with his head to convince the batter and opposition that he is shaking off the signal that the catcher has given him. In addition, the catcher may initially set up on the inside part of the plate or pound his glove near the batter and then at the last moment shift over to the outside part of the plate in order to deceive the opponent regarding pitch location. In some cases, veteran pitchers may have the autonomy to call their own game and relays signals to the catcher by using non-verbal cues, such as swiping down their leg with their glove. These tactics are used more commonly with a runner on second base, who may be relaying pitch signals in to the batter.

Q: 28. What signals will a pitcher show to his catcher in between innings to alert him as to which type of warm-up pitch is coming?

Lizzie Short

Lizzie Short

 A: Signals between the pitcher and catcher are devised so that the catcher is not crossed up and is able to successfully catch the pitch that is coming. In between innings, pitchers have up to five warm-up pitches to get ready for the upcoming inning. Therefore, it is important for the pitcher to determine which pitch he wants to work on or throw during this pre-inning warm up. As a result, he will use his glove to show whether a fastball, curveball, changeup, etc. is being thrown. For a fastball, the pitcher will swipe his glove forward. For a curveball, the pitcher will flip his glove-slide wrist over. For a changeup, the pitcher will move his glove back-and-forth. For a slider, he will move his glove horizontally in front of his waist. Typically, on the last pitch before the inning begins, the pitcher will throw a fastball from the stretch position.

Q: 29. Why will a base runner on first base sometimes look in toward home plate as he dashes to second base and other times not look in on his dash to second base?

Richard Paul Kane/Shutterstock.com

A: On a hit-and-run play, the base runner at first base will look in toward the catcher on his second or third step toward second base. The purpose of this glance is to see whether the batter has hit a ground ball or a pop-up, or has swung through the pitch. On a hit-and-run, the runner's job is not to steal the base, but to simply create movement that forces the middle infielders to cover the base and enable the batter to hit the ball in the vacated direction. On a straight steal, the runner must run full speed. As such, he should not do anything, such as turn his head, that might slow him down on his stolen base attempt.

Some coaches will time each of their base runners to see how long it takes them to run from their primary (8 to 10 foot) lead at first base to sliding in at second base. This time is compared with the pitcher's time to release the ball to home plate and the catcher's pop time to throw the ball to second base. If the base runner's time is lower than that of the combined catcher pop time and pitcher delivery time to the plate, then it is advantageous for the team to attempt a stolen base. As such, coaches can often be seen holding stopwatches in the dugout or in their back pocket as a base coach to acquire these times.

Q: 30. If a switch-hitter gets into the batter's box versus a switch-handed (ambidextrous) pitcher, who has to declare first which side they are pitching or hitting from?

Richard Paul Kane/Shutterstock.com

A: In the last 15 years, baseball has changed the rule regarding this situation. As such, a pitcher must determine which arm he is throwing with when a new batter enters the batter's box. At that point, a switch-hitter may opt to bat whichever way he sees fit. Typically, a switch-hitter will bat right-handed versus a lefty pitcher and left-handed versus a righty pitcher. Previously, the batter had to signal which side of the plate he was batting from, which dictated to the pitcher from which side he would throw. Although this is a rare situation, especially at the major-league baseball level, it is something that has occurred within professional baseball.

Q: 31. Why will a hitter sometimes smell his bat in the batter's box?

Lizzie Short

 After fouling off a pitch, hitters will occasionally smell the wood on their bat at the point where they typically make contact. When a batter fouls off a very fast pitch, it is possible to smell wood burning. As a result, hitters will sometimes grab the barrel of their bat and smell it before getting ready for the next pitch.

Q: 32. What is an "inside move" or "step over"?

Dennis Ku/Shutterstock.com

Dennis Ku/Shutterstock.com

Dennis Ku/Shutterstock.com

A: With a runner on second base, the pitcher may lift his stride leg as if he is delivering a pitch to home plate but, instead, spin or "step over" the pitching rubber and make a pick-off throw to second base. If the base runner is attempting to steal third base, he is likely to be caught in between second and third base, when the pitcher spins with his stride leg around to pick off to second base. It is likely in this scenario that a rundown will ensue after the pitcher throws to the third baseman, since the runner is caught in a pickle.

Q: 33. What is and provide an example of verbal obstruction?

STOCKMAMBAdotCOM/Shutterstock.com

 A: Verbal obstruction occurs when a player, typically an infielder, uses words to deceive the opponent. If, during an attempted stolen base, an infielder verbally calls to catch a make-believe high fly ball to confuse the base runner, it is deemed verbal obstruction and illegal. When called, the runner(s) are awarded an extra base. For example, during a game, an offensive team was able to steal numerous bases, because the catcher had a weak throwing arm. So, the coach had the catcher throw a pop-up toward the shortstop on stolen base attempts. The shortstop was instructed to wave his arms and yell, "I've got it," which was ruled as verbal obstruction.

34. What is the proper umpire call when the infield is playing in on the grass and the batter hits a ground ball that hits a base runner leading off first base?

Richard Paul Kane/Shutterstock.com

A batted ball that hits a base runner, who is not on a base, is typically ruled an out on the offense. However, if the infielders can all potentially make a play on the batted ball, then the situation is different. In the case of the infield playing up on the grass, a batted ball that travels past all of the infielders and then strikes a base runner is ruled a live ball. Given that the infielders all had an opportunity to make a play on the ball, the offense is not penalized for the ball striking one of their base runners.

Q: 35. In the USA, how many warm-up pitches is a pitcher allowed to throw before an inning begins? Is it the same number throughout the game?

Photo Works/Shutterstock.com

A: When a pitcher enters the game, including to start a game, he is entitled to eight warm-up pitches. All subsequent innings, he is allowed to throw five pitches before an inning begins. As a pitcher begins to fatigue and has accumulated a relatively high pitch count, he may choose to not use all of these warm-up pitches in between innings.

Q: 36. If a player misses a coach's signals, how can he signal to show that he wants them repeated?

Lizzie Short

A: When a player is on base, he may be distracted by a number of things, including the basemen holding him on, the first base coach, his teammates, or the fans at the game. His number one priority, after finding where the ball is, is to read the third-base coach's signals. If he misses part or all of the signal sequence, he may make a circular motion by extending his pointer fingers, which signifies that the coach should go through the signals again.

Many coaches can get frustrated if this scenario happens frequently, since it slows the game down, gives the opponent another opportunity to steal his signals, and demonstrates that the base runner may not have been paying attention. As a result, players may often not ask the coach to review the signals and therefore do not know if a particular offensive strategic play has been called on a given pitch.

Q: 37. What is the purpose of the little white pouch on the dirt part of the back of the pitcher's mound?

Lizzie Short

Lizzie Short

A: There are various rules that pitchers have to follow when on the mound and rubber. The rules vary according to the air temperature, precipitation, and the umpires' discretion. These statutes include blowing on their hands, licking their fingers, wiping off their fingers, and more. There are several tools/utensils that are commonly seen at the back of the mound on major-league diamonds, including a white pouch (a blue pouch for the Los Angeles Dodgers) of rosin, which enables pitchers to have a better grip on the baseball. Bowlers and basketball players are often seen using loose rosin to improve their grip on the ball.

On hot summer days when pitchers are sweating on their hands and arms, it is not uncommon to see a pitcher dab the rosin bag all over his arms and hands, so that he gets more traction on the baseball. In addition to the rosin bag, most fields will have a rectangular mat with bristles on it for cleaning the bottom of a pitcher's spikes. Some players will also use a tongue depressor for this purpose.

38. How do defensive teams defend or guard against a bunt?

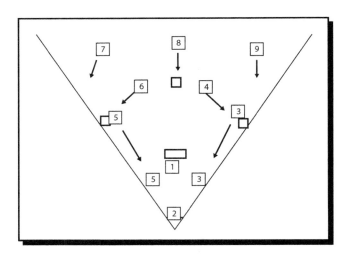

Third baseman charges in for the bunt. Shortstop rotates to cover third base. First baseman charges in for the bunt. Second baseman rotates to cover first base. Catcher communicates which base to throw to and who has the best angle to field the bunted ball. The ball is thrown to first base if there is no chance of getting the lead runner out. Left fielder backs up third base. Centerfielder backs up second base. Right fielder backs up first base.

When defensive teams expect a sacrifice bunt, they will often have their corner infielders (first and third baseman) charge toward the batter and have the middle infielders (second base and shortstop) rotate to cover first, second, or third base. This tactic is known as the "wheel play" or "scissors play," which is the most aggressive defensive strategy to defend the bunt.

Among the other strategies that may be employed in this situation are the pitcher covering the third-base line and the first baseman charging in to cover the first-base line. Alternatively, teams may have the third baseman charge in to cover the third-base line, while the pitcher covers the first-base line. All factors considered, these two strategies are more conservative, since there are fewer moving infielders and less chance for a mishap.

39. Why are there so many left-handed first basemen?

Daniel M. Silva/Shutterstock.com

A: Left-handed throwers are typically pitchers, first basemen, and/or outfielders. Due to the fact that infielders almost always throw to their left because that is where first and second base are located, left-handed throwers are at a disadvantage on the infield. First base is the only position where a fielded ball is thrown to the player's left. As a result, it is advantageous to have a left-handed first baseman. When fielding bunts and throwing to second/third base, tagging runners on pick-off plays, and throwing to second base for a double play, left-handed throwers have an advantage, because they do not have to turn their bodies as much as a right-handed thrower would have to in these instances.

Baseball is often described as "a game of inches." As such, having to turn 90 degrees to make a throw or tag play can be the difference between an out and a safe-call on a close play. Furthermore, more batted balls are hit to the left of the first baseman. As a result, for a lefty, a batted ball would be to a left-handed first baseman's glove-side, not to his backhand, which it would be for a right-handed fielder. Therefore, left-handed throwers do normally not play infield positions, other than first base.

40. Why do pitchers wear a jacket when running the bases?

Debby Wong/Shutterstock.com

In an effort to keep their throwing arms warm during a game, pitchers will call time-out when reaching base so that a bat boy or coach can bring a jacket to them. A pitching arm that cools down will tighten up and be less loose for throwing more innings within a game. It is also common for a pitcher to wrap towels around his arm in between innings to keep it warm and moist.

41. Aside from defending against a possible bunt, why does the third baseman sometimes jog in and out a few steps in the middle of an inning?

Lizzie Short

Lizzie Short

With a man on first base, the pitcher will intermittently make pick-off throws to the first baseman. When the first baseman makes a return throw to the pitcher, it is the responsibility of the third baseman to back up this throw. If the throw is wild or tips off the pitcher's glove, the base runner at first base can advance. As a result, it is customary for the third baseman to back up all of these throws.

42. Why can a manager call "time-out" and argue for a longer, more arbitrary amount of time than a coach in any other sport?

Dennis Ku/Shutterstock.com

Unlike all other major sports, baseball coaches are dressed in the same uniform as the players. Historically, baseball coaches were "player-managers," who not only coached the team, but were also integral players in the game. A manager or coach in baseball is allowed to call time-out and discuss rules, judgments, umpire positioning, and other aspects of a given play more than any other sport. While some of these differences concerning how points of contention are addressed are based on tradition, they are also due to the pace of the game. Basketball, football, hockey, and soccer all have running clocks and do not have coaches on the field. As a result, baseball coaches are in closer proximity to the umpires and can call time-out to stop a game, with less intrusion into the nature of the sport.

43. What should the on-deck batter be doing, while waiting for his turn at bat?

thomas m spindle/Shutterstock.com

While waiting for his turn at bat, the on-deck hitter should be studying the pitcher's delivery, including various pitches, his arm angle, and his timing. Players waiting to hit should also take note of the pitcher's pickoff move and his other mannerisms, so that they are ready when they're batting or running on the bases. In the case of a runner racing to home plate, it may be appropriate for the on-deck hitter to signal to which side of the plate the runner should slide.

44. What is the difference between a drag bunt and a push bunt?

DebWong/Shutterstock.com

A drag bunt is when the batter tries to bunt the ball to the pull-side and surprise the defense for a base hit. A push bunt on the other hand, is when the batter bunts to his opposite side in an attempt to stymie the defense and reach base safely. Therefore, a left-handed batter will push a bunt toward the third baseman and drag a bunt toward the first and second base area. For a right-handed batter, the opposite would be the case.

Q: 45. Why would a fielder purposely drop a pop-up or fly ball?

Don Purcell/Shutterstock.com

A: With a runner on first base, a middle infielder may choose to let a routine pop-up fall so that the team can turn a double play. In order for this tactic to work, the fielder will have to pretend that he is going to catch the ball and then at the last minute let the ball drop so that he can turn a double play. On a bunt that is popped up, the catcher can also elect to let the ball drop so that he can throw to the lead base for a force-out and turn a possible double play. If the lead-runner is very fast, it is advantageous to get a force-out and keep the speedy runner off the bases.

In another scenario, a corner outfielder (the left or right fielder) may choose to let a catchable fly ball land in foul territory so that the runner on third base cannot tag up and score on the play. Although the fielder will be declining to record an easy out, the runner on third base may represent the winning or go-ahead run.

46. When or why would a runner tag up at first base?

Lizzie Short

On a relatively deep fly ball to the outfield, especially to left field, a runner on first base may choose to tag up and advance to second base. This situation typically occurs on long, high fly balls in which the outfielder has a clear bead on a ball that will not go over his head for a double. During games, when stealing a base can be very difficult, this is a good strategy for a runner to get into scoring position on a fly ball.

47. How should a fielder grip a ball before throwing it?

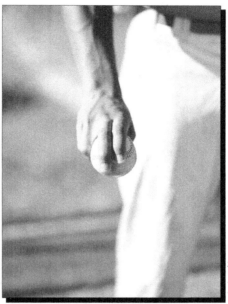

Lizzie Short

All fielders should grip the ball with a "four-seam grip." A four-seam grip enables the player to throw the ball in the fastest, straightest fashion. Pitchers, on the other hand, will use a variety of grips to deceive and disturb hitters' timing. Many players will utilize various drills that are designed to help them quickly grip the ball with four-seams, so that they can make a quick exchange from their glove to their throwing hand. Players are often seen in the dugout flipping the ball up in the air and grabbing it with their desired grip.

48. Why might an infielder or outfielder play a ground ball differently, if it is hit by the lead-off hitter, as opposed to the fifth batter in the lineup?

Brandon Vincent/Shutterstock.com

 As a rule, the first batter in the lineup (the lead-off hitter) is the fastest runner on the team. As a result, defensive players must field ground balls with a sense of urgency, so that the lead-off hitter, or any batter with excellent speed, can be thrown out at first base. This situation may require that the fielders change their positioning and/or charge the ball and get rid of it quicker with a speedy man at the plate. Conversely, with a big, lumbering player batting, infielders can play further back and not hurry their throws. As a result, scouting reports for the running speed and hitting tendencies of opponents, for example, and more have gained considerable attention in recent decades.

Q: 49. Why does the catcher only sometimes stand in the on-deck circle, waiting his turn to hit wearing shin guards on his legs?

Bill Florence/Shutterstock.com

With two outs, catchers often wait for their turn to hit, while wearing their shin guards. If the offensive inning ends, and they do not have any of their catcher's equipment on, it will often take too long for a catcher to put on his gear and get out to the field for the defensive half of the inning. Therefore, catchers will wear half of their equipment (the shin guards), while anticipating their turn at bat. If the batter in front of them reaches base safely, they will quickly take off their shin guards and bat. If he does not reach base safely, the catcher will put on his remaining gear and hustle out to catch the pitcher, as the next half inning begins.

In the case of a catcher batting or being on the bases when an inning ends, a backup catcher or coach will warm up the pitcher in between innings. With the slow pace of games gaining scrutiny in recent years, catchers tend to be more aware about quickly getting their gear on and hustling out to their position.

Q: 50. Why do middle-infielders (shortstops and second basemen) wear the smallest gloves/mitts on the field?

Lizzie Short

A: The larger the glove a player uses, the longer it will take him to get the ball out of the glove to make a quick throw. As a result, catchers and middle infielders use the smallest gloves on the field, given that they have to release the ball faster than any player on the team. Second baseman and shortstops will try to turn double plays or nab hitters on close plays at first base. Similarly, catchers must quickly get the ball out of their glove to throw out base runners attempting to steal. While they are giving up glove size and a few inches of range to catch a ball, they are gaining quickness in transferring the ball from their glove to their throwing hand.

51. What is the *backdoor play*?

Aspen Photo/Shutterstock.com

The backdoor play usually occurs on a ball hit to the shortstop's backhand where he does not have a play on the runner at first base. Instead of throwing to first base, he uses a long-armed fake throw to first base, spins around, and throws to third base, trying to catch a base runner who has over-rounded the bag. This play is usually implemented with a runner on second base at the time of the pitch. More often than not, this runner will be overly aggressive as he rounds third base and looks to score on an errant throw by the shortstop to first base. By faking the throw to first, the defense and shortstop will have a better opportunity to surprise the base runner at third base. While other infielders can utilize the back door play, it most often occurs with the shortstop, who has a longer throw and tends to be more athletic than the other fielders.

Q: 52. What is a *Baltimore chop*?

Dennis Ku/Shutterstock.com

A Baltimore chop is when a batter hits a ball straight down on the ground that takes a high bounce, which the infielders have a difficult time fielding, before the batter is able to run safely to first base. The name derives from the hard infield dirt in Baltimore, where batted balls would bounce with a high trajectory, making it difficult for the defense to make a play on them. During the dead-ball era of the late 1800s, Baltimore was known for inserting cement in front of home plate, so that their hitters could purposely hit pitches directly down at the ground in that area to produce a high chop and beat it out for a single.

53. What is a *Texas Leaguer*?

Eric Broder Van Dyke/Shutterstock.com

When a batter hits a ball that falls in between the infield and the outfielders, it is known as a "Texas Leaguer." These hits are not hit hard or with much authority. Instead, they are soft "dinkers" or "bloops" that land in front of the charging outfielder. The name derives from 1901, when rookie Ollie Pickering was called up from minor league baseball in the Texas League and proceeded to hit seven consecutive bloop singles to start his MLB career [Mlb.com]. Another theory claims that the term comes from a team in the Texas League that intentionally hit bloop singles to reach base. Yet, another point of conjecture is that the expression derived from the situation in which the fierce winds from the Gulf Stream knocked down fly balls for singles in the Texas League [Seattlepi.com].

Q: 54. What is *the neighborhood play* and will instant replay make it obsolete?

Eric Broder Van Dyke/Shutterstock.com

On ground balls that are likely to be double plays, the middle infielders do not have to actually touch second base before throwing to first base. Rather, they simply must be in the vicinity or "neighborhood" of the base. This rule was implemented so that the second baseman and shortstop could avoid being spiked or injured by the incoming base runner sliding into second base.

Umpires will not reward infielders with being in the neighborhood, if the infielder does not make the throw to first base, or if the feed to the second base area pulls the base man away from the base. Since the inception of instant replay, infielders are judged more strictly on how they turn double plays. As a result, the neighborhood play is expected to be extinct in future years.

55. What is a *double-switch*?

Bill Florence/Shutterstock.com

The double-switch substitution that managers make occurs primarily in the National League. In the later innings, after a starting pitcher has come out of the game, coaches will utilize their bullpen. Many of these pitchers only throw one to two innings. It is commonplace to replace them in the batting order with a position player who hits more effectively, because when the pitcher is near his turn in the batting order, it makes strategic sense to hit for him with a position player. In order to complete a double-switch, coaches will typically replace the pitcher with an outfielder, and then replace an outfielder with the next pitcher whom they will be putting into the game. By using this double-switch technique, managers can move the batter hitting for the pitcher higher up in the lineup and also ensure that the inserted pitcher is in a batting slot that is relatively far away from where they are currently in the batting order.

Q: 56. What is the rag or giant ChapStick-looking tube that hitters often rub on their bats before hitting?

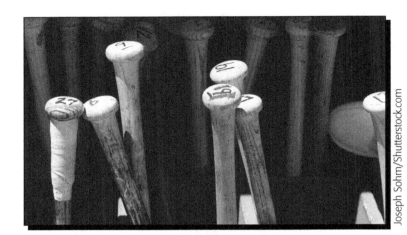

Joseph Sohm/Shutterstock.com

When a manager inserts a pinch-hitter into the lineup, it is common to see that hitter warm up very quickly, before taking his turn in the batter's box. This warm-up may include him swinging a weighted bat or metal pipe, and rubbing something on the handle of his bat. As a rule, this rubbing consists of a sticky substance that will give him a better grip on the bat. Traditionally, pine tar is rubbed on the bat with a leather pouch the size of a legal pad. Other options include a sticky stick that is rubbed on the bat like ChapStick on lips.

Players who use pine tar liberally can be spotted with discolored helmets, bats, and sometimes dirty shoulders. As a hitter, resting a pine tar covered bat on your shoulder while waiting for a pitch, will leave a dark stain on the uniform. In reality, there are players who like to have the look of a dirtied, hard helmet and uniform.

Hall of Famer, Kansas City Royals' player George Brett hit a home run against the New York Yankees during the 1983 season, which was highly controversial and became known as "The Pine Tar Game." After touching home plate, the Yankees appealed the home run, because the pine tar was higher on the bat than legally allowed. The umpire measured the length of pine tar on the bat and ruled Brett's home run illegal, and, therefore, called him out. In an infamous display of emotion, Brett ran out of the Royals' dugout screaming with his arms flailing and argued with the umpire.

The Royals subsequently protested the game, and American League President Lee MacPhail upheld the protest. Brett's home run was restored and the game was replayed from the time of the home run. The Royals ended up winning the game 5-4 [SI.com; July 23, 2016].

Q: 57. Why do so many pitchers get hurt and require arm surgery?

Aspen Photo/Shutterstock.com

A: Over the course of the last decade or so, there have been an exorbitant amount of arm injuries, primarily among pitchers. These injuries, in most cases, involve the UCL (ulnar collateral ligament), an injury that typically leads to a procedure that is also known as Tommy John surgery. While the single culprit is not definitively known, contributing factors include an undue reliance on strength training, and a year-around involvement with the radar gun, which motivates pitchers to pitch with a max effort or a throw with a 90-mph mentality. In that regard, many teams, including the Major Leagues and squads all the way down to Little League baseball, are monitoring the number of pitches that are thrown and number of days of rest in between performances. On the other hand, the mentality of trying to throw as hard as possible on every pitch must change, if these injuries are going to subside.

58. How can a manager protest a game (file a protest)?

Richard Paul Kane/Shutterstock.com

Managers can only file a protest during a game, when there is a rule that is broken by an umpire's call. Poor umpire judgment is not sufficient cause to protest a game, but an umpire call or ruling that contradicts a pre-existing baseball rule is grounds for a manager to protest a game. For example, if a base runner slides into home plate and is clearly safe, and the umpire calls him out, this is not grounds to protest the game. If an umpire calls a balk, however, and advances the base runners two bases, instead of one, the coach or manager may protest the game.

59. What is a first-and-third defense?

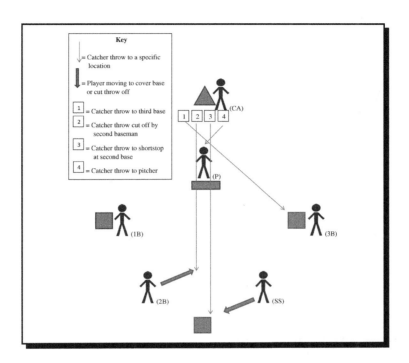

With runners on first and third base simultaneously, the defense must decide how they will react if the runner on first base attempts to steal second base. If the defensive team has a large lead, or if the runner is slow, they may opt to throw to second base to nab the base stealer. On the other hand, if the game is tied, or if the runner at first base is an exceptionally fast runner, the defense may not throw at all. Alternatively, the catcher can fake a throw to second base and throw to third base or throw the ball back to the pitcher. Some teams will defend the first and third base steal by having the shortstop cut off the catcher's throw to second base and then throw to home plate, if he sees the runner leave from third base.

60. Why would a MLB manager expect a base runner to sprint from second base to home plate on a base hit, especially with two outs?

Bill Florence/Shutterstock.com

A runner attempting to score from second base on a base hit can be a crucial run in a game. If he does not cross home plate before the batter is tagged out on a base hit with two outs, the run does not count. If the batter is out on a force play, then this scenario is irrelevant. On the other hand, if the batter hits a single, tries to advance, and is out on a tag play, then the runner approaching home plate must score before the runner is tagged out. Otherwise, his run does not count.

Q: 61. Why might a MLB manager not expect a hitter to sprint to first base after hitting a routine ground ball on the infield, no matter how many outs there are?

Dennis Ku/Shutterstock.com

A: Although high school and college coaches expect their players to sprint down the first base line every at bat, the same factor is not true for Major League managers. Given the length and exhaustion of a 162-game season, MLB players are not expected to exert themselves every time they hit the ball. While fans sometimes view this mindset as lazy or lackadaisical, the players are trying to save their legs and bodies for the rigors of a long season. Baseball often gets ridiculed for being a non-contact sport and/or one that requires limited physical fitness. The stop-and-go nature of the game, however, creates a great deal of aches and pains, especially from running hard.

Q: 62. Can a pitcher spit on his hand and then "rub up" the baseball? Can he rub the ball in the dirt? Can he blow on his hand?

Lizzie Short

Lizzie Short

A: Umpires and coaches will typically discuss ground rules before the game, including what the pitcher is allowed to do in terms of "going to his mouth." On cold days, for example, pitchers are often allowed to blow on their hands. If pitchers put fingers in their mouth, in general, they then have to wipe their hand on their uniform afterwards. During the 2017 post-season, Chad Morton of the Houston Astros was seen touching the bubble gum in his mouth, which perhaps created an improved, sticky grip on the baseball. This act caught the attention of his opponent, the New York Yankees, who addressed the situation with umpires. Baseball pitchers throughout history have been found guilty of using various substances to "doctor up the baseball," including Vaseline, spit, sandpaper, and pine tar. They have also utilized other devices and substances in an attempt to improve their grip or cut the ball to aid in gaining movement on their pitches.

63. Why will a hitter sometimes tap the top of his helmet in the middle or beginning of an at bat?

Lizzie Short

When a hitter steps into the batter's box, calls time-out, and then taps the top of his helmet, he is asking for the base umpire to move his position. Hitters want to be able to focus on the pitcher and not have distractions in their line of sight, when they are trying to focus on the task at hand.

64. Why might a batter be hit by a pitch and not be awarded first base on a "hit by pitch"?

Aspen Photo/Shutterstock.com

If an umpire deems that a batter purposely let a thrown pitch hit him, he can rule that the pitch was a strike and/or make the batter stay in the box and not be awarded first base. If the batter is down in the count (e.g., 0-2; 1-2), he may intentionally let a pitch hit him. In particular, an inside curveball that won't hurt his body is an ideal pitch to let hit him and earn a free pass to first base. With all of the arm guards and equipment that players now wear, it is less painful to let a thrown pitch hit their body. During the 1971 season, Ron Hunt of the Montreal Expos set a MLB record by getting hit by a pitch 50 times in a season. Although not a man of large stature, Hunt was known for crowding the plate and letting pitches hit his body. His remarkable feat is 43 percent more than any other player attained in one season in history. Few records in any sport are held by an individual, in this instance, who has a 43 percent lead on the second-place athlete behind him [https://fivethirtyeight.com/features/the-year-ron-hunt-got-hit-by-50-pitches/].

Q: 65. What is *defensive indifference*?

Eric Broder Van Dyke/Shutterstock.com

A: Quite often at the end of the baseball game, the defense is fixated on securing their victory. When a base runner attempts to steal a base, the defense may not even throw to second base to try and record an out. In these instances, the official scorer rules this as "defensive indifference." The defense is indifferent or uninterested in the base runner, because they either have a large lead or do not want to make a mishap when attempting to throw out the base stealer.

Q: 66. What is a *slide-step*?

Dennis Ku/Shutterstock.com

When a base stealer is on first base, the pitcher must make sure that he does not get too big a jump and steal second base. In addition to making pickoff attempts to first base, he should try to have a quick delivery to home plate, so that the catcher has a realistic opportunity to throw out the base stealer. One strategy for doing this is to utilize a "slide step." The slide step is when a pitcher does not lift his stride leg up too high and quickly delivers the pitch to home plate. Because the pitcher is trying to get the ball to the catcher in 1.3 seconds or less, he does not have time to use a high leg kick.

Q: 67. What does it mean to *step in the bucket*?

mTaira/Shutterstock.com

A: Many young hitters struggle to stride straight toward the pitcher, when they're hitting. This may be the result of a fear of being hit by the baseball or a lack of confidence that they will be quick enough to get their bat through the strike zone when swinging. In turn, these batters may step out or toward the first and third base line, as left-handed and right-handed hitters, respectively. This movement is commonly referred to as "stepping in the bucket." The name derives from a drill that coaches used many years ago to correct this problem. Coaches would put a bucket full of water next to a hitter's front foot, and if he stepped out, his foot would get wet as he stepped "into the bucket." As such, coaches often use feedback drills, such as this one, to try and change the bad habits of their players.

Q: 68. Name four types of fastballs.

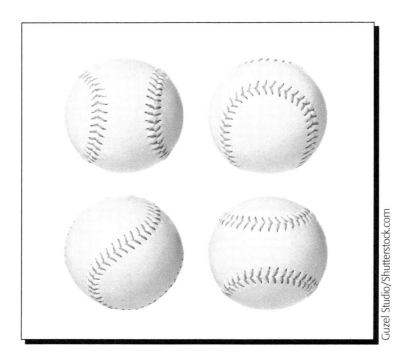

Guzel Studio/Shutterstock.com

A: The most common type of fastball is known as the four-seam fastball. This particular fastball is thrown with the middle and pointer finger draped across each of the four seems on a baseball. The pitch is delivered in the straightest, fastest fashion of all pitches. The two-seam fastball is thrown with the pointer and middle finger hanging over two seams on a baseball, which creates a downward, sinking movement to a pitch. The cut fastball is a pitch that cuts or moves across the plate, much like a slider. Lastly, the split-finger fastball is a pitch in which the pitcher separates his pointer and middle finger on the baseball and throws a pitch that dives or drops during the last few feet as it arrives at home plate.

Q: 69. What is a *hanger*?

mTaira/Shutterstock.com

In baseball terms, a "hanger" is when a pitcher throws a breaking pitch that does not break. Furthermore, the pitch is up in the strike zone and gives the batter an opportunity to drive the ball effectively, since it is at eye level and has little or no movement on it.

70. Why do catchers often look up at the hitter's face and eyeballs while giving the pitch signals?

Greg Kushmerek/Shutterstock.com

Hitters may use their peripheral vision to sneak a peek at the catcher's pitch signals, which will give the hitter an advantage when facing a pitcher. As a result, catchers are commonly seen looking up at the batter's eyes while flashing pitch signals to the pitcher. In some cases, catchers may threaten a batter with a fastball directed at his head if he tries to look down at the pitch signals.

71. Why are there so many players with arm and leg guards?

Rena Schild/Shutterstock.com

Much like a warrior entering combat, there is an abundance leg, arm, and other protective equipment that players wear during competition. These guards help fend off fastballs that hit them on various parts of their body, especially the arm, when facing pitchers. Because foul balls are also hit off various body parts, protective devices are worn for player protection of their shins and feet. All-in-all, the underlying purpose of wearing these implements is more to limit the prevalence nagging injuries throughout the course of the season.

72. How come pitchers rarely throw complete games?

DebWong/Shutterstock.com

Arguably, the greatest change in baseball over the last 50 years has been the increased reliance on relief pitchers. Traditionally, starting pitchers would not only complete a large percentage of the games, they would also pitch several times per week. In recent years, it is commonplace for starting pitchers to expect to throw only five or six innings and then have the bullpen finish the game. There are specialists for the sixth, seventh, eighth, and ninth innings, which enables managers to maneuver their pitching staff, according to the specific situation at hand. With statistics such as saves, holds, and more, coaches can match up pitchers against specific batters and evaluate probable outcomes. It is difficult for batters to hit for as high a batting average, given that a new pitcher often comes in for the second half of the game, almost in every inning, throwing 95 miles an hour or faster.

Q: 73. Why are there so many strikeouts in the modern MLB?

Aspen Photo/Shutterstock.com

A: Throughout most of history, hitters have been taught to shorten up their swings and put the ball in play with two strikes on them. During the last decade, this philosophy has changed. More and more hitting coaches are encouraging their batters to get lift on the ball and swing the bat with an upswing trajectory in order to get backspin on the ball. While these swings can generate tremendous power, they also lead to many swings and misses. This mindset, combined with pitchers who are throwing harder and harder every year, equals a record number of strikeouts in recent seasons. Furthermore, with pitcher specialists who pitch one inning or less per appearance, batters have to face pitchers who are throwing 95 mph fastballs or faster. Lastly, with advanced scouting on hitters' hot and cold zones, hitter weaknesses are more exposed in the modern era. In short, the game has changed to a point where home runs and strikeouts are the norm, while singles, stolen bases, and "small ball" are the exception.

In 1927, teams averaged just three strikeouts per game. By 1952, the average had reached four per game. The number climbed to five in 1959 and six by 1994. In 2010, teams averaged seven strikeouts per game, and the number rose to eight by 2016 [*USA Today*, September 28, 2017].

74. Is it wrong for a team to keep scoring and stealing bases, when they have a large lead?

stephenkirsh/Shutterstock.com

Baseball teams have historically considered it "bush league" to continue scoring runs, after obtaining a substantial lead on their opponent. Stealing bases, bunting, and playing aggressively to score more runs after getting a lead of 7 to 10 runs, for example, has always been considered taboo. Teams that do that are scorned by their opponents and may expect the opposing pitcher to throw pitches at their batters in retaliation. Other individuals, however, feel that no lead is a safe lead. They also believe that the trailing team should just play baseball as best they can and not worry about the scoreboard or let it dictate the nature of their play.

Q: 75. What/where is the strike zone?

Jeff Smith - Perspectives/Shutterstock.com

A: While many baseball enthusiasts gauge the strike zone on a batter as the area from the knees to the letters, it varies, depending on the umpire. In fact, some umpires may have a smaller strike zone, some umpires may have a lower strike zone, and some umpires may have a wider strike zone. All-in-all, the strike zone may be determined by the height or personal preferences of a specific umpire. The key component in determining an umpire's effectiveness is his ability to make consistent ball/strike calls throughout a game, regardless of his particular preference. Umpires who are inconsistent or change their strike zone from inning to inning will inevitably be ridiculed, while those umpires who have a tendency to call strikes in a certain way that they maintain throughout the game will be deemed as effective.

Q: 76. Why do players slide headfirst into first base?

Lizzie Short

Research studies have shown that sliding into first base headfirst or footfirst is actually slower than running through the base standing up. Nonetheless, it is still common for players to dive headfirst trying to beat out an infield single at first base. The only time it makes sense to dive headfirst into first base is when a player is trying to avoid a tag by the first baseman, who may have come off the base to catch an errant throw and must tag the base runner. Many players will dive headfirst into first base as a means for showing off their hustle and gritty play. In the end, however, it only increases the risk for injury and slows their efforts to get to first base in the fastest means possible.

Q: 77. Why do players slide headfirst into home plate?

A: When a player slides into home plate, he is approaching and making contact with a catcher who is wearing hard gear. As such, it would seem that diving headfirst into home plate is not advantageous. By diving headfirst into home plate, however, base runners have the opportunity to maneuver their hands to swipe the plate, as they make a fade-away slide to avoid a tag. While a fade-away slide can be utilized by sliding footfirst, moving their hand back-and-forth to touch home plate is much more effective.

Q: 78. Why do players leave their fielding gloves in a specific location in the dugout?

David Lee/Shutterstock.com

A: When an offensive inning ends, players on the bases go directly to their defensive position. Before doing so, a player or coach must give them their glove. To make this process more systematic and organized, position players leave their fielding gloves in a specific spot in the dugout, so that they can "pick each other up," if and when a player is left on base as an inning comes to an end. For example, all three outfielders will keep their gloves together in one spot in the dugout, so that any one of them can grab the gloves and bring them to their fellow outfielders, who are left on base when an inning ends.

Infielders will use a similar procedure to ensure that every fielder is brought their gloves, if they are on base when an inning ends. In addition, centerfielders and first baseman are typically responsible for bringing a baseball with them out to the field for use during pre-inning warm-ups.

79. What is a "small ball" game strategy?

Aspen Photo/Shutterstock.com

"Small ball" tactics include bunting, stealing bases, utilizing the hit-and-run, and other aggressive techniques that are aimed at scoring one run at a time. This method or philosophy has a higher risk of creating an out. Although many teams in the MLB score the bulk of their runs via extra-base hits or home runs, there are still those managers and teams that use running speed and unpredictability at bat to score runs. This strategy is particularly effective against dominant pitchers, especially during playoff baseball, when most teams tend to have several very talented frontline pitchers.

80. Why would a catcher purposely not catch a pitch?

Ken Durden/Shutterstock.com

 When a defensive team is frustrated with an umpire's ball/strike calls, there are a number of tactics they can take to address their feelings. Most commonly, the catcher will ask the home plate umpire where a pitch missed the strike zone, without turning his head or body around—which might show up the umpire publicly. In other instances, the pitching coach or manager may make a visit to the mound and, as the umpire approaches him to break up the mound visit, he will discuss the pitch or pitches that were in question. If all else fails, a catcher may, on occasion, purposely not glove a high fastball that will intentionally hit the umpire. On September 13, 2017, the Detroit Tigers were accused of this tactic. In turn, their manager Brad Ausmus and catcher were ejected from the game.

Q: 81. What is a *check-swing*?

Elias H. Debbas II/Shutterstock.com

A check-swing occurs when the batter is indecisive concerning whether to swing at a pitch. In the process, he may attempt to stop his swing and not offer at a pitch. At the MLB level, which employs a four-umpire system, the umpires on the first and third base line have a good view of whether the batter "broke the plane" and actually swung at the pitch. For example, with a right-handed batter hitting, the umpire on the first base line has a good angle to see the plane of the batter's swing path. These calls van be very difficult, since not only is the umpire over 100 feet away, but the batter often comes very close to crossing through the strike zone with the barrel of his bat, when he's offering at the pitch.

Q: 82. What is the hidden ball trick?

Bill Florence/Shutterstock.com

A: The hidden ball trick involves an infielder holding a baseball at his side and attempting to tag a base runner, who thinks that the infielder does not have the baseball. Typically, this will occur after a pickoff throw or an outfield throw to a cutoff, man whereby the base runner may be tricked in to thinking that the pitcher has the baseball. By rule, the pitcher may not be standing on the pitcher's mound for a player to be called out on a tag play in this situation. While these plays happen infrequently, they create excitement and large momentum swings within a ball game, when they actually occur.

Q: 83. What is *double-play depth*?

Dennis Ku/Shutterstock.com

A: When the shortstop and second baseman play at double-play depth, they stand closer to second base and the batter. This positioning increases the probability of the infielders having time to field a ground ball, flip or receive a throw at second base, and make an effective throw to first base, before the batter gets there. While this strategy can prevent them from ranging to ground balls in the hole, it enables them to have a better opportunity to turn a double-play.

84. What is an *unassisted double play*?

Aspen Photo/Shutterstock.com

When a player fields a ground ball, line drive, or pop up to compile two outs on his own, it is considered an unassisted double play. He is responsible for recording the outs without anyone else touching the baseball. Most commonly, this occurs on line drives where the fielder snares a hard smash in the air and then quickly tags the base runner or the base closest to him for the unassisted double play. When the offensive team uses the hit-and-run-play, they are susceptible to the defense catching a line drive and "doubling up" the runner on first base with an unassisted double play.

85. Who decides which pitch to throw: the catcher, pitcher, or coach?

Bill Florence/Shutterstock.com

Historically, the only reason catchers flashed signals between their legs was to make sure that they wouldn't get crossed up on a pitch that the pitcher was going to throw. As a result, traditionally, it was the pitcher's decision to determine which pitch would be thrown. Once advanced scouting reports became commonplace, however, many teams began calling pitches from the dugout by relaying pitch signals to the catcher. As such, hitters often display certain tendencies and weaknesses that can be exploited by a coach who targets those tendencies by signaling for specific pitch location/type.

There are teams and coaches, however, who believe that the catcher should learn how to pitch to batters and "call the game." Much of this decision-making is based on the philosophy of the manager in charge. In addition, veteran ballplayers, especially pitchers, usually have autonomy to decide which pitches are thrown.

86. What is a *double-cut*?

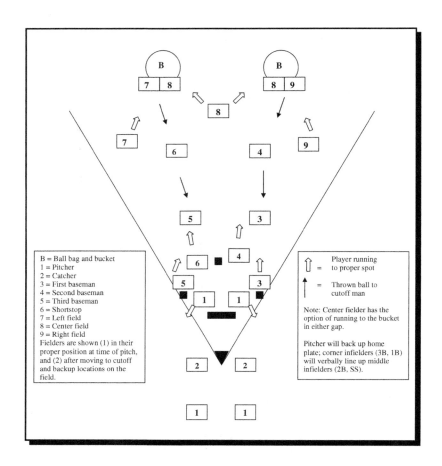

When balls are hit to the outfield fence down the line or in the gaps of right-center and left-center field, two infielders are typically used to set up cutoff throws. These throws are between the outfielder who fields the ball and the catcher/third baseman who ultimately receive the throw. When the ball is hit down the left-field line, the shortstop and third baseman will be the cutoff men between the leftfielder and the catcher. This enables the middle infielders to redirect the throw, if there is a misguided throw or when a situation is developing on the bases. In Major League Baseball, where player arms are so strong, double-cut plays are less common. In addition, with so little time to practice, teams rarely execute effective double-cut plays on balls that are hit to the most caverness locations on the field.

Q: 87. Why do infielders sometimes play on or move closer to the foul lines?

 A: There are situations during a game when the defense wants to avoid giving up a double. Perhaps, the winning run is on first base, or they want to keep the batter (who represents the tying run) off of second base. In these scenarios, the first and third basemen will play closer to the line to prevent a double being hit down the line. Furthermore, outfielders will play at a more conservative depth, as well.

Q: 88. What is the *five-man infield*?

Eric Broder Van Dyke/Shutterstock.com

A: With the go-ahead run on third base, some defensive teams will intentionally load the bases. At which point, they are hoping to get a force-out at home plate and/or turn a home-to-first double play. In rare instances, a manager may move one of his three outfielders into the infield to increase the likelihood of fielding a ground ball and getting the lead runner out at home plate and/or turning a double play. While this tactic is an aggressive defense alignment of the infield, it leaves a vacant hole in the outfield for certain routine fly balls. This alignment has a fielder at third base, shortstop, second base, and first base, as well as an additional player, who stands directly on or behind second base.

During the ninth inning of the 2008 World Series, manager Joe Maddon utilized a five-man infield by pulling his leftfielder in to play third base. Maddon has also implemented a four-man outfield in his coaching career [Espn.com; Jayson Stark; May 6, 2011].

Q: 89. What is an *over-shift* or *shift*?

Eric Broder Van Dyke/Shutterstock.com

A: An over-shift is implemented by the defense when it expects the batter to hit the ball to the pull-side of the field. For example, with a left-handed pull hitter batting, the infielders will shift over to the right-field line and position the third baseman in the shortstop area, while the shortstop plays where the second baseman would typically play. During this shift, the second baseman will cover shallow right field, expecting a hard line drive or a ground ball to be hit in that area. In recent years, this defense has become used regularly, as many hitters are reluctant to make adjustments and hit the ball to all parts of the field.

Year	Number of MLB Over-Shifts
2013	9,437
2014	17,152
2015	19,417
2016	30,938
Chart courtesy of MLB Network, Bill's Blackboard, March 21, 2018	

Q: 90. What is an *unintentional intentional walk*?

Bill Florence/Shutterstock.com

A: With an open base, i.e., there is a runner on second base, and no one is on first base, many defensive teams will pitch around the batter, knowing that a walk will not advance the lead runner. In other instances, they will intentionally walk (automatically put the batter on first base) a hitter who is feared.

By unintentionally intentionally walking a batter, the defense is simply not throwing him any good pitches to hit. As a result, he is likely to walk to fill the open base at first base. If he does swing, the batter will likely hit the ball weakly for an out, given that the pitcher is purposely throwing pitches out of the strike zone.

In putting the batter on first base, the defensive team is setting up a force-out at all bases, as well as a double play situation. If the next batter hits an extra-base hit, the walk will be deemed a mistake, since multiple runs will score.

Q: 91. Why would a pitcher want to vary his timing and not deliver pitches with the same pace every time?

Keeton Gale/Shutterstock.com

A: When a pitcher varies his timing and delivers the ball to the plate in different sequences of holding the ball, stepping off the mound, and shaking off signals, it can disturb the batter's rhythm. With a runner on base, it makes sense for the pitcher to be unpredictable in terms of his timing to home plate. This tactic can make the runner on base uneasy, with regard to trying to time the pitcher and get a good jump to steal a base. Therefore, a pitcher who is predictably unpredictable and varies his looks and moves to the plate, disturbs both the batter and base runner(s)' timing effectively.

92. Why might hitters (or their coaches) decide that they should "take a strike" before swinging?

Dennis Ku/Shutterstock.com

By taking a strike and not swinging until a pitcher throws a strike, batters can make pitchers work harder. As a result, pitchers will run higher pitch counts and may pitch fewer innings. In addition, batters will be less fooled by a pitcher's arsenal of different pitches, if they see more pitches per at bat. The strategy of taking pitches may be particularly effective, when an opposing team has a limited number of relief pitchers or a tired bullpen. It should be noted that some hitters are innately free-swingers, while other hitters are more comfortable running deeper counts and hitting with two strikes on them.

Offensive teams will have their players take a strike, when they are trailing by a sizable margin, or if the pitcher is wild and is struggling to throw strikes. Some coaches will have batters take a strike as a tactic to draw walks, especially when a weak hitter is at bat.

Q: 93. Why are coaches often seen looking at binders in the dugout?

Lizzie Short

DebWong/Shutterstock.com

A: Baseball managers and their assistant coaches frequently look through binders in the dugout. These binders contain scouting reports, charts, and other data involving matchups between specific hitters and pitchers. In addition, many of these charts also detail batter tendencies concerning where a particular better usually hits the baseball. These "spray charts" are often used to dictate how teams will move their fielders to defend against each batter.

Ultimately, this data may prompt coaches to pinch-hit for a batter or to bring in a relief pitcher for a specific situation. Some managers rely more heavily on these scouting reports, statistics, and "analytics" than others. Other managers use their gut instincts to coach in a more traditional manner by letting the game situation dictate their coaching decisions.

Q: 94. Why do infield cutoff men sometimes catch throws from the outfielders and other times purposely let them go by?

Aspen Photo/Shutterstock.com

A: The purpose of an infield cutoff man is to provide the proper alignment and a target for the outfielder. In addition, the cutoff man may redirect a throw to a base, when the defense has a better opportunity to record an out against an advancing base runner. It is important for the cutoff man to not cut outfield throws that are on target. These accurate throws will get to a fielder covering the base more quickly for catching and making a tag on an incoming base runner. Defensive teams should communicate on how to let outfielder throws go through and not be cut on plays like this.

On other plays, the outfielder throw may be offline or need to be redirected, based upon how the base runners are advancing in the developing situation. At the Major League level, much of this is practiced during spring training. As a rule, during the course of the season, teams do not usually rehearse these plays.

Q: 95. What is a *walking lead*?

Eric Broder Van Dyke/Shutterstock.com

Eric Broder Van Dyke/Shutterstock.com

A: Base runners at second and third base will typically utilize a walking lead. This tactic enables them to create momentum toward the next base by getting their feet started, as the pitcher begins to deliver a pitch to home plate. Unlike at first base, where the base runner must be ready to move in either direction and stands relatively stationary, runners on other bases can have active feet. At first base, the pitcher is closer to the base runner and has a better opportunity to pick him off with a pickoff throw. This is less realistic at second base, where the base runner can take a walking lead, because not only is it a longer throw for the pitcher, but the fielders are not stationed to the base, like at first base.

At second and third base, the runner can keep his feet in motion and start his move toward the next base. When stealing third base, many runners will improve their quickness and attain their top running speed sooner by implementing a walking lead.

96. What does it mean to *go up the ladder*?

"Wait until I put my hand over his eyes,
and then throw your fastball."

Cartoon Resource/Shutterstock.com

When a batter chases high pitches, many pitchers will "go up the ladder." When doing this, the pitcher will throw fastballs that may be at armpit height, the neck, or hitter eye level. This strategy is typically used when the batter is behind in the count, e.g., 0-2 or 1-2. Some hitters have a tendency to go fishing for pitches up in the strike zone. Furthermore, there are pitchers who possess an effective high fastball or have a knack for throwing a rising, neck-high fastball that entices batters to chase after.

Q: 97. How does a pitcher earn a *save*?

Anthony Correia/Shutterstock.com

A: One of the very important statistics that baseball keeps track of is the "save." To earn a save, a pitcher must enter the game with the tying run in the on-deck circle. For example, during a 5-3 game, with a man on first and a new pitcher enters the game, it is a save situation. In the MLB, the closer only pitches in a game when it is a save situation, or if he has not pitched in a while and needs some work to stay fresh.

Q: 98. Why are the players always chewing?

Bill Florence/Shutterstock.com

DebWong/Shutterstock.com

A: It has always been a baseball tradition, wherein players and coaches chew bubblegum, tobacco, and/or spit sunflower seeds. With all the down time during a baseball game, these activities keep players busy. There are also people who believe that chewing gum and tobacco relaxes the jaw and, as a result, relaxes the whole body. This sense of loosening up can be important when hitting, pitching, and performing on the baseball diamond. Tobacco products have been banned at all levels of baseball, except on the professional level. Gum, sunflower seeds, and other snacks come in pouches and cylindrical tins that mimic the packaging of tobacco products.

Q: 99. What is a *12-6 curveball*?

Dennis Ku/Shutterstock.com

A: Just as there are several types of fastballs, pitchers throw different varieties of curveballs. The 12-6 curveball breaks in a downward fashion, from the top to the bottom of the strike zone or "nose to the toes" (of the batter). A 12-6 curveball refers to the hands on a clock, with the "12" at the top and the "6" at the bottom. A curveball can also slide across the strike zone on a 10-4 angle, as well as on other angles in that range.

Rich Hill of the Los Angeles Dodgers features at least four curveballs in his arsenal that vary in both velocity and the angle of break. Early in the count, slower curveballs are more commonly thrown, so the pitcher can get ahead of the batter. Later in the count, harder curveballs and sliders tend to be more prevalent.

100. What is *pepper*?

John Kershner/Shutterstock.com

Pepper is game that players have played since the origin of baseball in the 19th century. Before games begin, batters like to swing a bat and make contact with thrown balls. Not only does pepper enable players to do this, it also warms up their glove action/throwing arms. To play pepper, players will stand with their gloves in a semicircle formation and throw pitches to one player who is batting. The batter takes a short, half-swing and hits ground balls to the players in the semicircle.

Pepper games can have a variety of rules, including one that stipulates that any batted line drive that is caught on the fly by one of the fielders results in an out for the batter, who must then give up his turn at bat and join the fielders. Pepper has been banned at MLB ballparks, because it tears up the grass near the home plate area and leads to batted balls that risk hitting fans in the first few rows of the stands.

How to Determine Your Baseball IQ

Step 1.   Raw Score: add up how many correct answers you scored out of 100
(_____/100)

Step 2.   Baseball IQ Score: multiply the number of correct answers by two
(_____/100 x 2)

Step 3.   Baseball IQ Range: use the scoring chart below to find your Baseball IQ
Classification

Baseball IQ Scoring Chart

Baseball IQ Range	Baseball Intelligence Classification
181-200	Baseball genius
165-180	Baseball near-genius
149-164	Very superior baseball intelligence
133-148	Superior baseball intelligence
117-132	Above-average baseball intelligence
85-116	Average baseball intelligence
69-84	Below-average baseball intelligence
52-68	Borderline baseball deficiency
Below 52	Baseball deficiency

About the Author

Since 1992, Darren Gurney has been coaching NCAA and high school baseball. Gurney has coached over 20 players who were selected in the MLB Draft or that have gone on to play professional baseball. Some of these players include: Tom Koehler (Miami Marlins), Sal Iacono (Houston Astros), Steve Gilman (Detroit Tigers), and James Lasala (New York Yankees). With coaching tenures at Division I Iona College, The New York Cadets of the ACBL, New Rochelle High School, and Keio Academy, Gurney has been named "Coach of the Year" three times and also selected as field manager for the ACBL Collegiate All-Star Game.

In 1998, Gurney founded the Rising Star Baseball Camp, which has helped develop and place players in numerous college baseball programs. Rising Star graduates have played in various powerhouse programs, such as St. John's, Stony Brook, Villanova, Duke, Elon, University of Pennsylvania, LeMoyne, University of Massachusetts, Mt. Olive, Franklin Pierce, and more.

Gurney is the lead analyst for the progressive website: TheBaseballDoctor.com. Through video reviews and analysis, Gurney has helped professional, amateur, and youth players across the world improve their hitting/pitching mechanics. In 2015, the Baseball United Foundation forged an agreement with Gurney to provide Internet-based video hitting instruction to players in Pakistan, Croatia, Ireland, Uganda, Nigeria, Iran, and Nepal.

As founder of Ultimate College Prep, Gurney is the director of a college preparatory baseball program for players ages 17 and 18. This program has helped foster recruitment for dozens of players in NCAA baseball teams, including Elon, Stony Brook, Notre Dame, Iona, Fordham, Seton Hall, Rhode Island College, Columbia, and more. These intensive and comprehensive workouts along with the creation of recruiting videos/DVDs help market and prepare players for the college baseball experience.

In 2017, Coach Gurney began coaching for Team America with USA Baseball Coach Peter Caliendo. He coaches USA Travel Baseball Teams that play competitive teams throughout the world, including Japan, Dominican Republic, Cuba, and other historic, culturally stimulating travel destinations. During the August 2017 trip to Tokyo, Japan, three Rising Star Campers played for him and represented their country.

Currently, Gurney coaches at Keio Academy in Purchase, New York. Keio is a Japanese boarding school with a rich baseball history, including two New York State baseball championship game appearances in the last 10 years. More recently, in 2016, the team won the NYS Section One championship game 2-0 at Boulder Stadium in Rockland, New York.

Like many coaches, Gurney started his career as a player. As a four-year varsity letterman at Washington University, he compiled a .389 batting average and a .542 on base percentage in Conference UAA competition. Gurney realized his dream when he was signed by the Hard Bulls in Austria of the European Professional Baseball League in March, 1995. He continued his career for the next 11 years with the Pleasantville Red Sox as centerfielder and was inducted into the Hall of Fame in November 2005.